TC

D1606776

DISCARD

# Nature's Children

# BIRDS OF PARADISE

### Irena Hoare

GROLIER
EDUCATIONAL

Ed
De
Bird
ISB
1. Bir
QL696.P
598.8/65

# FACTS IN BRIEF

## Classification of Birds of Paradise

| | |
|---|---|
| Class: | *Aves* (birds) |
| Order: | *Passeriformes* (songbirds) |
| Family: | *Paradisaeidae* |
| Genus: | There are 20 genera of birds of paradise. |
| Species: | There are 43 species of birds of paradise. |

**World distribution.**   The island of New Guinea and small islands nearby. Four species are found in northern Australia.

**Habitat.**   Forests, particularly in mountainous areas.

**Distinctive physical characteristics.**   Short legs; large, strong feet; beaks vary from short and stubby to long and slender; loud voices; males often have brightly colored feathers and long, ornamental plumes.

**Habits.**   Stay close to home and do not fly far. The males are noted for their courtship displays during the mating season.

**Diet.**   Berries, fruit, insects, and seeds. Some species eat small mammals, birds, and reptiles.

© 1999 Brown Partworks Limited
Printed and bound in U.S.A.
Editor: James Kinchen
Designer: Tim Brown

**Published by:**

GROLIER
EDUCATIONAL

**Sherman Turnpike, Danbury,
Connecticut 06816**

**Library of Congress Cataloging-in-Publishing Data**

...ds of Paradise.
    p. cm. -- (Nature's children. Set 6)
    ... 0-7172-9353-X (alk. paper) -- ISBN 0-7172-9351-3 (set)
    ...ds of Paradise--Juvenile Literature. [1. Birds of Paradise.] I. Grolier Educational (Firm) II. Series.

...26H635  1999
...-dc21
                                                                98-33402

# Contents

If you ever wanted to see a live bird of paradise, you would need to be very adventurous. They live mostly high in the trees, in dense tropical forests where few people live. There are few paths in these forests, so you would need to find your own way. Then you might have to sit still for hours before seeing a bird of paradise, because they are shy and keep hidden from view. Luckily, some adventurous people have had the patience to observe these beautiful creatures. Let's read on and find out some of the things they have discovered.

*Perched high in a forest tree, the lesser bird of paradise of Papua New Guinea displays its magnificent tail feathers.*

## A Name for a Mystery

Opposite page:
*A sixteenth-century illustration of a bird of paradise.*

Many centuries ago, when the first Dutch merchants began to trade in New Guinea, strange stories were told about the mysterious birds that were found there. The traders did not see any live birds, but the people of the islands offered the traders the birds' skins in exchange for other goods. The legs had been removed from the skins, but the bird's beautiful feathers were carefully preserved.

When the traders got home, people were impressed by the glorious plumage of the birds. They were also puzzled that they seemed to have no legs. A story grew that the birds never landed on the ground but flew constantly around the sun until they died and fell to Earth. It was said they ate no food but just drank dew.

When it came to naming these amazing footless birds, the story of how they never came to Earth stuck in people's minds. It was the Dutch who called them the birds of paradise—do you think it suits them well?

## Family Connections

It's hard to believe, but the bright and beautiful birds of paradise are closely related to the crow family. They are in the family of crowlike birds called the Paradisaeidae. It is such a huge family that it is divided into many smaller subfamilies. The bird of paradise subfamily contains 43 different species.

You may not think birds of paradise are much like crows, but they do all have some features in common. For example, they nearly all like to stay close to home. They also have strong feet and toes (for grasping branches), strong beaks—and very loud voices.

There are so many species of bird of paradise that scientists have listed them in groups. Among others, there is a long-tailed group, a long-billed group, and a group in which the males help care for the young.

*This male Raggiana bird of paradise is hopping sideways on a branch before he begins his courtship dance.*

## Where Are They?

The birds of paradise live mostly on the large, hilly tropical island of New Guinea, which lies off the north coast of Australia. The island is covered with thick forest, which is where the birds often live high up in the treetops.

Some parts of New Guinea are very hard to reach. You have to go through jungle without paths and cross swamps and mountains. A lot of the birds live in these remote places. They hide well and are hard to see, and scientists still have a lot to find out about them.

Some birds of paradise live on small islands dotted in the Pacific Ocean close to New Guinea. Four species are found in northern Australia. Some of the birds can be found only in one very small area. For example, the red bird of paradise lives only on the tiny island of Waigeo, off the northwest corner of New Guinea.

*Victoria's riflebird is a bird of paradise that lives in the rain forests of Queensland, Australia.*

MacGregor's bird of paradise likes to live in the damp environment of cloud forests.

## High Life and Low Life

Birds of paradise like many different habitats, even though they all live in or near New Guinea. All the different kinds of bird have found what suits them best. The Raggiana is often seen in casuarina trees, close to villages. The sickle-crested bird of paradise prefers to live high in the mountain forests. MacGregor's bird of paradise is happy when it is higher still, in damp cloud forests up to 13,350 feet (4,000 meters) high. Lawes' parotia likes to live in mountain oak forests, and the king bird of paradise confines itself to lowland forests.

## Heard But Not Seen

It is very rare for humans to see some species of birds of paradise. This makes it all the more exciting when you catch a glimpse of them through the trees.

One of these elusive birds is the blue bird of paradise. It keeps itself well hidden, although its call is often heard. Those who have seen the male say he is one of the loveliest sights of New Guinea. He hangs upside down to try to attract females. As soon as he is hanging head down, he shakes himself and spreads out shining blue plumes, and dances the plumes up and down. He lets his long tail streamers form a graceful arc over the cascade of blue feathers, and all the time he sings a soft song.

*New Guinea cloud forests are the home of the blue bird of paradise.*

# Bird Alert

If you lived in New Guinea, you would see some birds of paradise, such as the greater bird of paradise, quite often. They are seen, and certainly heard, all over the island. Other species are more rare. They like only a few kinds of food and a few kinds of nesting place. It is important that people do not change these areas too much, or the birds might die out.

Goldie's bird of paradise is one of these rare species. They live in the hilly rain forests of the Fergusson and Normanby Islands. The King of Saxony species is also in danger. It lives in the mountain forests of central New Guinea. The forests are being cleared because people need land for farming, but this could be a disaster for the birds. Bird-lovers all around the world are working hard to try to solve this problem.

*King of Saxony birds of paradise like this one are under threat as their rainforest homes are cut down.*

## Sizing Up

Think of a starling, then think of a raven, and you will know roughly the size range of the birds of paradise. The smallest species is the crimson-red king bird of paradise, which is about five and a half inches (14 centimeters) long. The largest species is the ribbon-tailed bird of paradise. These birds look extra long because of their two central tail feathers sweeping behind them. The feathers are almost 39 inches (one metre) long or about three times as long as the bird's body. In most species males are a little larger than females.

All the birds have short legs and large, strong feet. They prefer to stay close to home and do not fly far. Because they fly mostly from branch to branch, they need sturdy legs so they can cling on tight to trees.

In contrast, the beaks of the birds of paradise vary a lot. Insect-lovers have long, strong bills, good for crunching hard on beetles. The birds who feed by sucking nectar from flowers have slender bills.

*The female buff-tailed sicklebill bird of paradise has an unusually shaped bill, which she uses to feed on nectar from flowers.*

# Feeding Time

Birds of paradise are always looking out for food, so they never stop hopping and flying about. They are the liveliest birds you can imagine, in constant motion all day long.

Most of the true birds of paradise will eat either fruit or insects, and these birds are called omnivorous. The fruit-loving birds keep their eyes open for figs or seeds and berries. The king bird of paradise is tiny, but it likes to eat the largest fruits in the jungle. The insect-lovers like to gobble up grasshoppers, locusts, or cockroaches. The ribbon-tailed bird of paradise will even eat small mammals and amphibians, such as frogs and newts.

*Victoria's riflebird loves to feed on fruit in the Queensland rain forest.*

## Sounds Loud

If you like the cawing sound of the crow, you might like some of the harsh noises made by birds of paradise. They make a variety of calls, but few of them are musical. Some birds of paradise also like to mimic sounds.

Although it is rare to see many birds of paradise in the wild, it is very common to hear them. The insistent cawing of the male Raggiana as he calls for a mate is well known in the New Guinea jungles. Other species make all sorts of sounds. The call of the Lawes' parotia is a powerful barking growl—"graa graa"—while that of the blue bird of paradise is a mournful, ringing note. The greater bird of paradise can often be heard, loud and shrill, over a wide area, and the riflebird's hiss sounds like a bullet hurtling through the air.

*The call of the male Raggiana bird of paradise is well known in New Guinea. These birds can also learn to mimic sounds.*

*The male trumpet manucode bird of paradise has blue iridescent head feathers.*

# Fine Feathers

The feathers of a male bird of paradise can be crimson red, bright moss green, golden yellow, or deep purple. No wonder these birds like to show off! The females, however, lack the bright plumage of the males.

Some of the male birds are mainly black, with patches of bright, glimmering feathers. Others are colored all over, with areas of red, blue, green, or yellow. Even the inside of the birds' mouths may be brightly colored.

As well as their ordinary feathers, male birds of paradise have special ornamental ones. These are often very long, with elegant curls at the end. Others are fluffy and can be fanned out into amazing shapes. Some species have strange thin, very long feathers with bright tips. These are called "wires" and can grow from the head or the tail.

## Amazing Plumes

The fantastic feathers of the male birds of paradise are one of the marvels of nature. Among the most strange are the two head feathers of the King of Saxony bird. They are about 18 inches (45 centimeters) long, divided into 30 or 40 blue segments, and look like a row of small flags. It is hard to believe they belong to a little bird the size of a thrush. Although it is the same size, the male King of Saxony bird is brighter than a thrush, with a yellow belly and striped wings.

The male Wilson's bird of paradise has two amazing tail feathers. They are blue, and each curls around into a large circle. On the bird's neck is a tuft of yellow feathers, which fluffs up into a bright halo. The bird's back is scarlet, and its breast is a dazzling green.

The male Lawes' parotia has six mobile "wires" that grow like a crown, as well as a wave above its head. The bird has shimmering blue-green breast feathers, which it fans out to make a bright shield.

*The male lesser bird of paradise displays its beautiful long tail feathers.*

# Fan-tastic

There seems no end to the shapes a bird of paradise can make with its feathers. The male superb bird of paradise makes a large fan that springs up and out from the back of his neck. He displays a fan-shaped shield on his breast at the same time.

When the male twelve-wired bird of paradise is trying to attract a mate, he spreads out a wide blue-green collar all around his head. He fluffs out bright yellow plumes at his sides at the same time.

The male Wallace's standard wing bird creates a specially beautiful shape. He spreads out the green shield on his breast and raises four delicate ornamental feathers from his back. They make a lacy pattern over his head and fluffed-out wings.

*This male Wallace's standard wing bird of paradise shows off his green chest feathers.*

## A Patchy Phase

Until he is a year old, a male bird of paradise looks just like a female—brown and quite dull. Then he starts to molt and loses some feathers at his head and throat. He looks a bit patchy for a while, and then, little by little, these feathers are replaced by colored ones.

The next time he molts, his new tail and head feathers begin to grow longer than the rest. Later still, more brown feathers are replaced by bright tufts and side plumes. The male birds must molt at least three times to gain their brightly colored feathers. Birds of paradise molt once a year, so males are over four years old when they reach full splendor.

The birds find it quite hard to fly with such long feathers, so they usually do not fly very far. They have just had to accept that beauty has its drawbacks.

*Female birds of paradise lack the beautiful plumage of the males.*

# Plume Pillage

Almost 500 years ago the first traders from the West landed on the large island of New Guinea in search of spices. They must have been amazed by the exotic plant and animal life they saw. Among the sights would have been the beautiful feathers of the bird of paradise, perhaps in the headdresses of the tribespeople. The native people of the island have used the feathers as decoration and as a form of money for many hundreds of years.

European sailors certainly brought bird of paradise skins back to Spain in 1522, and a lively trade in the feathers quickly grew. In the last century fashionable women in Europe liked to have bird of paradise feathers in their hats, and this led to thousands of these beautiful birds being killed. Fortunately, it is now forbidden to hunt them, so today they can live in safety in the forests.

*A Melpa tribesman from Papua New Guinea sports bird of paradise feathers in his headdress.*

## A Place to Show Off

In order to find a mate, most male birds of paradise rely on the glossiness, brightness, and beauty of their plumage. The birds love to show off these plumes, and each species displays in a different way.

Most birds of paradise display in trees, but some species display in a dancing area on the ground in forest clearings. These areas are called arenas. Different species make different sorts of arena.

If you catch sight of a male bird of paradise hopping around in the treetops, tearing off twigs and leaves, you might think he is building a nest. Or if you see one rooting around on the ground, moving leaves and stones, you might think he is looking for food. But if it is the mating season, he is probably making an arena in which he can display his fine feathers.

*The Raggiana bird of paradise likes to display his fine feathers on the branches of trees.*

*The male satin bowerbird favors the color blue and decorates his bower with any blue object he can find, such as feathers and berries.*

# Houseproud Cousins

Because of the arenas the male makes, the bird of paradise is called an arena bird. A close cousin within the family of crowlike birds is the bowerbird—also an arena bird. They may not look like close relations, but there is only one important difference between these cousins. Instead of growing beautiful feathers with which to show off, bowerbirds have learned to build highly decorated arenas, called bowers.

The bowerbirds take the building of an arena several steps further than the birds of paradise. For example, they may build an "avenue" of twigs or a tall pile of sticks up to 10 feet (three meters) high in their arena—just to make it look good. Some birds may even carpet their arenas with fresh green leaves.

These cousins show how two families of birds can develop in different ways, although they start from a common beginning.

# Choose Me!

Some birds of paradise, such as Raggiana birds of paradise, like to display their fine feathers and dazzling colors in large groups. The Raggianas' display is seen quite often, because these birds like to be near humans. They sometimes live in trees on the outskirts of villages.

The males display in "leks," or dance trees. There might be as many as 10 birds on one tree, though each one has his own special perch. He clears away any leaves that might hide him and fights other male birds who come too close to his perch.

When the males have prepared their trees, the female Raggianas appear, and the males all show off their glorious plumage. They stand still with their wings open. Then they fluff up the mass of their bright orange feathers, like a shower of flames behind their yellow heads. They wait while the female decides which one looks the finest. She shows which one she likes best by sidling up close to him.

# A Delicate Courtship

The display of the Lawes' parotia takes place on the forest floor. The bird hops around, removing twigs and stones. He clears the leaves from nearby trees so the sun can make his feathers gleam. He chooses some perches and strips them of leaves and bark. When he is satisfied, he leaves but comes back to tidy his dance area every day.

When a female arrives, the male bird flaps his wings at her. If she flies off, he knows she was not looking for a partner. If she remains, he enters the arena and lets out a cascade of velvety black side feathers. They stand out like a skirt, all around his front. His six long head wires, with their shining tips, are flipped forward over his face. Then he dances, delicately shaking his head.

# Nesting Times

If you were a baby bird of paradise, you would probably be living in a nest built by your mother. This is because it is usually the female bird of paradise who builds the nest and looks after the young. In a few species the males help build the nest and feed the chicks. The males in these species are less colorful, such as the Loria's bird of paradise.

The females usually build their nests in trees. Their cup-shaped nests are made of grass and leaves. The nest of the king bird of paradise nest is different—it is just a hole in a tree.

Although most birds of paradise nest in trees, not quite all of them do. Multicrested birds of paradise build elaborate nests on sticks near the ground. The nests are mossy and round and have a roof.

# How Did It Happen?

The tropical forest, where the birds of paradise live, is a wonderful environment for them. They have few enemies, and there is plenty to eat. In these pleasant conditions they can breed freely. This is why, over millions of years, so many colorful species have evolved.

The birds of paradise do not mate with one partner and bring up their chicks as a couple. Instead, most males have many partners. The females like only the loudest and most colorful male birds. So the males keep having to prove they are the best of the bunch.

The male with the brightest plumage gets the most partners. His male offspring, too, tend to have brilliant feathers, and they pass these on to the next generation. As this keeps happening, even more spectacular species evolve. Some of them are so fantastic, it is hard to believe they are real.

*Lush tropical rain forest provides an ideal habitat for the many bird of paradise species.*

## Family Life

A baby bird of paradise is quite likely to be an only child, because the mother birds often lay only one egg. Sometimes they lay two, so the chick may have one brother or sister, but rarely more than that. The mother usually guards the egg, or eggs, alone, sitting on them to keep them warm for between two and three weeks. She goes off to seek food for herself, but comes back quickly to keep the eggs safe.

Once the little chick arrives, the female bird of paradise busily flies around finding it food. The babies stay in the nest for up to 30 days, eating food that has first been chewed up by their mother. The chicks are quite helpless at first, but they are soon able to spit out fruit stones from the nest—a sure sign that they are growing up.

# Words to Know

**Arena**   A space that a male bird clears for himself, in which he can show himself off and attract a mate.

**Display**   To show off beautiful feathers or make dancing movements in order to attract female birds.

**Environment**   A place that provides food, water, and shelter, allowing different creatures to grow and survive.

**Habitat**   A place in which a particular animal, plant, or bird can usually be found because the conditions are right for them.

**Lek**   A tree in which male birds of paradise display.

**Mating season**   The time of the year when male and female birds come together to produce young.

**Molt**   To shed old, worn-out fur or feathers in preparation for growing new fur or a new set of feathers.

**Omnivorous**   Able to eat both animal and vegetable foods.

**Perch**   A place, often a tree branch or twig, on which a bird can stand and rest.

**Plumage**   All the feathers together on a bird.

**Plumes**   Another word for feathers.

**Wires**   Very thin, long feathers, which can grow from a bird's head or tail.

# INDEX

**Cover Photo:** Michael S. Yamashita / Corbis
**Photo Credits:** Eric and David Hosking / Corbis, page 4; The Academy of Natural Sciences of Philadelphia / Corbis, page 7; Bruce Beehler / NHPA, pages 8, 12, 19, 23, 24, 39; Pam Gardner; FLPA / Corbis, pages 11, 31; A.N.T. Photo Library / NHPA, pages 15, 20, 36; Michael S. Yamashita / Corbis, pages 16, 27, 35; Morten Strange / NHPA, page 28; G. I. Bernard / NHPA, page 32; Jack Fields / Corbis, page 42; Wolfgang Kaehler / Corbis, page 44.

$$2\overline{)48}$$
$$\underline{48}$$

FC